The Art of Longing

Poems by

Robert A. Neimeyer

With artistic contributions by

Richard Knowles
Lisa Jennings
Alfonso Garçia
Barbara Thompson
Todd Hochberg
and
Sigrun Menzel

Layout by Jessica van Dyke

Cover art: *Between Worlds,* 2007, acrylic and mixed media, by Lisa Jennings

ISBN: 1-4392-2611-3
ISBN-13: 9781439226117

Visit www.booksurge.com to order additional copies.

CONTENTS

ABOUT THE AUTHOR

Robert A. Neimeyer

Robert A. Neimeyer is a practicing psychotherapist and the author or editor of 22 books, including *Meaning Reconstruction and the Experience of Loss* (American Psychological Association), *Constructivist Psychotherapy* (Routledge) and *Rainbow in the Stone*, a book of contemporary poetry (Mercury). A professor of Psychology at the University of Memphis, Neimeyer travels widely as a popular workshop presenter, integrating art as well as science in his training on grief and human resilience. His poetry appears in several journals, in both the humanities and the helping professions.

ABOUT THE CONTRIBUTORS

Richard Knowles

Richard Knowles is a Mid-South painter with an extensive record of exhibitions, commissions, and teaching. He is a retired Professor of Art (Distinguished Emeritus) from the University of Memphis who continues to produce paintings, drawings, and photography for exhibition at many local, regional, and national sites. He is represented in collections and installations in Boston, St. Louis, Kansas City (KS),Little Rock, Nashville, Memphis and other city museums, universities and private collections. He is represented by the Jay Etkin Gallery in Memphis.

Lisa Jennings

Lisa Jennings is a professional sculptor and painter living and working in Williamson County, Tennessee. Her paintings are multi-layered, multi-media works and her sculptures are made from found wood and stone. She exhibits year-round in galleries throughout the Mid-South and her works have been acquired for private, corporate and permanent museum collections.

Alfonso Garçia

Alfonso Garçía currently works in cut iron and steel sculpture in a medium and large format in his home in Santa Cruz de la Palma, Spain. His open-air installations strive for a dialectical exploration of the landscapes in which they are grounded, while also expressing a life of their own.

Barbara Thompson

Barbara Thompson is a licensed clinical social worker, occupational therapist, and associate professor in The Sage Colleges Occupational Therapy Program. She has a certificate in post graduate studies in the expressive arts from the European Graduate School, and incorporates art-based approaches in both her teaching and private psychotherapy practice. A lover of dreams and the sea, her work combines images from both seen and unseen landscapes.

Todd Hochberg

Todd Hochberg is a professional photographer who works in conjunction with hospital bereavement programs and palliative care services to produce legacy photographs and videos for families grieving the death of a loved one. His work is part of the permanent collection of the George Eastman House International Museum of Photography and has been featured in *Life* magazine, the *Chicago Sun-Times* and numerous other media and professional publications. More information about his work can be found at www.toddhochberg.com.

Sigrun Menzel

Sigrun Menzel, born in 1958, works as an artist and clinical psychologist in Osnabrück, Germany. She is best known for her series of open air installations entitled "Perlen Kullern" [Rolling Pearls], which draw attention to natural landscapes and flora in fresh ways. More information about her work can be found at www. sigrun-menzel.de.

Carol Knowles

Carol Knowles is an art critic for the *Memphis Flyer*, writing reviews of significant exhibitions in the Mid-South area by local, national, and international artists. Formerly an attorney and psychiatric counselor, she now spends her free time in literary pursuits and traveling with her husband, painter Richard Knowles.

FOREWORD

Like ancient seas that scour the land and grief that scours the heart, poet Robert Neimeyer's starkly beautiful collection of verse, The Art of Longing, takes us deep into the earth, deep into the heart of millennia of humans burying their dead, studying the stars, attempting to understand the universe and themselves. Neimeyer sets the landscape of our journey with his poem, Climbing Down, as we are "swallowed deep in the throat of rock" where "ancient seas wash the earth like a scouring hand … rise hot within us … bleed back into the raised ribs of earth, flowing yellow as bleached bones."

The remarkable images that accompany each of Neimeyer's poems include Lisa Jennings' textured, shrouded mixed-media-recreation of Ireland's sylvan landscapes, Barbara Thompson's oceanic watercolors, Alfonso Garçia's collaged homages to life, Todd Hochberg's simultaneously dark and luminous photography, Sigrun Menzel's intricate soft sculpture, and the crashing/jagged acrylics, oils and watercolors by Richard Knowles, a painter whose turbulent, nearly animate abstraction heightens our sense of being "swallowed deep in … rock."

Like Neimeyer's poetry, the artists' images are vivid and layered with meaning. Knowles' jagged shapes, thick ochres and umbers, streaks of red near the center of many of his paintings, and his titles—including Collapsing Cliff, Nautilus, and The Ethics of Paint—suggest complex, powerful emotions as well as geologic rift and upheaval. The nearly sheer rock face that fills Knowles' acrylic, Canyon Colorado Plateau, captures the element of danger involved in climbing down into earth, down into ourselves.

Many of the images in The Art of Longing are abstract or nearly so. Lisa Jennings scumbles and scrapes layers of acrylic paint and handmade paper into surfaces that look as textured and ancient as the limestone cliffs, the stone megaliths and Neolithic tombs she paints. Jennings heightens the sense of mystery by shrouding her landscapes in the ever-present mists of the Irish coast, what the ancients called the "veils between the seen and unseen worlds," and what Neimeyer describes in his poem, Mist, as the scene that "composes itself, / asks nothing, permits anything, / winds forward with its own rhythms."

Rhythm runs the gamut in these poems and images—from the "heart resting between beats" in The Meeting to the "pulsing of blood" in The Life Aquatic to a "shiver of feeling" in Mariza to Knowles' Collapsing Cliffs to the driving sexuality of When We Had Them. The urgency and immediacy of lovemaking are reinforced by the first line of Neimeyer's second, third and fourth stanza—"We did not think … we did not pause … we did not imagine."

A psychotherapist as well as a poet, Neimeyer conducts grief and transition workshops around the world. In his workshops, in his poems and in the images included in The Art of Longing, Neimeyer explores the ways we react to life, to loss, to our own mortality.

In Survivors a daughter's sudden suicide precipitates a mother's withdrawal from the world: "She has pulled in, and in / away form the pain… / she slips inside the sleeve of her music … / draws down into the bubble of her hope."

In Knowles' evocative visual narrative, Sunday Morning, a woman reads under bright, artificial kitchen lights absorbed in a newspaper. On the right side of the painting a man smokes, bends over a coffee table covered with glasses of coffee and beer. Both figures are oblivious to the deep-turquoise and midnight-blue forest that surrounds them.

During the last stages of his wife's illness, Alfonso Garçia created collages that suggest this couple embraced the universe as well as each other. A delicately rendered anatomical drawing of the ligaments and muscles of a man's chest, neck and face lies at the center of two of these works. Here is the artist laid bare. Every fiber of Garçia's being strains up and to the right. In Mi Cabeza, 9 he looks toward a heart imprinted with his and his wife's fingerprints. Above and below the heart Garçia writes, respectively, "Amor" and "Vida." In Mi Cabeza, 5, the artist's head, crowned with swirling stars, looks up at a planet floating in white space.

In a harrowingly beautiful memento mori, Neimeyer pairs Knowles' Shiva III with Cleaning Fish, a poem in which a woman "burned dry by the chemo" slices open a trembling fish with "white flesh/marbled through with crimson strands.../weedy womb overfull." At the center of Shiva III, a god's firm thigh and arched foot dance the cycles of life and death. Like the fish eaten by the woman whose body is eaten by cancer—Shiva's entrails, layers of flesh, and brachiations suggesting limbs and bones—morph into one another as life feeds off life.

Neimeyer is determined to embrace all of life — its pleasure and its pain—like the mothers who cradle their stillborn babies in Hochberg's untitled poignant photographs, like the companions in Neimeyer's poem, Travelers, who "taste the sweetness in the grapefruit's bite," and like the renowned Portuguese singer, Mariza, who harnesses life's energy and rides its storms: "Song made flesh/ you light the night with your eyes.../The fado breaks from you like a sudden gale. /In the swelling waves of your voice/ the sea rises like passion,/ falls hard upon the shore." The waves in Knowles' acrylic on paper, Wash Surf 4, also "rise like passion." They crash in all directions, spill over the edges of the painting and, like Knowles' geologic abstractions, they inundate us. There are no mark-overs, no whiteouts in the multiple washes that Knowles lays down with assurance—each spray, wave, and gesture is crisp and clean. Occasional dark passages suggest drop-offs where sea gouges deeper into earth.

Barbara Thompson's combination watercolor and pastel, In Situ 2, takes us all the way down. Jagged shafts of umber thrust our point of view across and down a tall lean painting in which turquoise gives way to purple gives way to midnight-blue. At bottom right, in water blurred by our rapid descent, we can just make out the yellow-green vegetation of the sea-bed.

Another poem, Poets' Workshop, also takes us down where deep in the human heart Neimeyer captures the complex love/hate relationship that exists between the novice writer and the mentor whose pronouncements can empower or destroy. In an overarching metaphor that never feels forced or artificial, Neimeyer compares the workshop experience to the novel, Moby Dick. By turns passionate, fearless, and mutinous, the young writers learn to be Ishmael, the storyteller who makes sense of life's chaos. They learn to be Ahab, the relentless pursuer of the Great White Whale, Neimeyer's fitting metaphor for the blank page, the white canvas, the idea and the feeling just beyond reach.

All the ideas and images inform and deepen one another, including Neimeyer's powerful pairing of his title poem The Art of Longing with Jennings' Between Worlds, an artwork that appears inside as well as gracing the book's cover. In Jennings' simultaneously personal, iconic and monumental work, a sunlit megalith morphs into the silhouette of a woman standing in shallow water, her feet planted in the ocean floor, her head turned to the right gazing further out to sea. Next to the figure is a currach, an open hide-covered boat that transported the ancients between coastal islands. Its golden oars nearly touch the luminous figure. The currach stands ready to carry the artist, the poet, the reader deeper into sea and soul. In poem after poem and image after image, Neimeyer's haunting explorations of life's great pleasures and great pains ask the reader a question: Will you, like the narrators in the poem, The Art of Longing, "nurse the hurt, refuse the fullness/of this world" or will you climb into the currach and ride the waves?

Dr. Carol Knowles
Art reviewer,
Memphis Flyer

PREFACE

Many readers of this collection of contemporary poetry will recognize that in my "day job" I work as a psychotherapist, scholar and trainer with a deep interest in grief and bereavement, so that encountering my work in the present context may strike them as anomalous. What, they might ask, is a psychologist doing writing verse, given the world he habitually inhabits? But in fact the span to be bridged between these two domains is less wide than one might guess, as my scholarly work over the last 30 years and my poetry over a much briefer period have come to explore similar terrain: our fragile attempts as human beings to organize a meaningful world in concert with others; the insistence of language; the tension between transcendence and constraint; the inevitable encounter with loss, and—less predictably—reconstruction. Thus, the free verse I share with friends and colleagues in personal correspondence, in workshop readings, and occasionally in print represents a thematic and substantive extension of familiar concerns about the human condition that will be recognized by many readers of my more academic work. As the constructivist psychologist George Kelly once implied, literary treatment of a topic can complement the scientific, and still be, in a sense, continuous with it.

But poetry can also offer something that theoretical, empirical or expository writing does less well, or at least less vividly, namely confront the reader (and often the writer) with what Kelly might call fresh "elements" of experience—pithy, poignant or perturbing glimpses of a personal, social or natural world that invite (or challenge) our meaning-making efforts. At the level of process, I also find points of difference, as well as similarity, when I shift my writing efforts from the computer keyboard on which I compose all of my "professional" work to the paper-and-pencil with which I tease lines from my poetic muse. Although both forms of writing flow best when I am feeling inspired and minimally directed by preconceived goals (which I take as something of a general principle for therapy and life as well), poetry requires something more: a clearing of mind, a slowing of pace, a patient opening to experience, cultivating a kind of "connoisseurship" for its novelty, feeling tone, contradiction. When the writing is going well it comes in short bursts of images, with half-conscious attention to alliteration, rhythm, prosody—factors that also play a role in my academic writing, but which are promoted to center stage when my focus is poetic. Something about this process makes me keenly aware of the dialectic between myself and the world, as I quiet my typically intense activity to "sit with" a memory, feeling, scene, perception, while also noticing its reverberation in me at nearly a bodily level. The mood is clearly an invitational one, bidding words to come, often in a way that surprises me, as I hope they might also surprise a reader. Forcing language on the experience is always deadly, producing just the sort of mechanical animation of an idea one would expect. Experientially, poetry feels like it is as much about "finding" meaning as "making" it—or perhaps better, about letting *it* find *me*. Ironically, this quiet cultivation of a poetic receptivity ultimately gives way to intense editing, as I comb through the lines to remove the tangles, cut and shape what remains, invite the critical eye of fellow poets—all steps that are conspicuously absent in my academic writing, which nearly always emerges unplanned and unedited, and goes to press just as it is written. When I consider the much greater editorial effort I exert to produce a one page poem than a 30 page article, I am reminded of Mark Twain's comment to a friend at the beginning of a long missive, to the effect that he was sorry to send such a long letter, but he didn't have time to write a short one!

The present collection of poems benefits enormously from their pairing with a series of images contributed by a handful of artists who I am fortunate to call friends. The project literally arose in conversation with them, and symbolically represents an extension of our conversations about the multiple messages of our respective work, whether rendered in the ephemeral medium of language, in the somewhat more substantial media of paper or canvas, or—in one instance—the durable medium of sculpted steel. In each case the poetry and artwork were created as freestanding pieces with their own integrity, rather than fashioned as linguistic or imagistic "commentary" upon the complementary work appearing alongside it. In a sense, then, the pairings arose from a sense of "resonance" between some features of the artwork and its accompanying verse, whether of a literal or more abstract kind. We hope that the visual, auditory, semantic and metaphoric associations triggered by these conjunctions open the receptive reader to deeper contemplation of both works, whose ripple effect perturbs, excites and perhaps occasionally affirms a responsive reading of their meaning.

Robert A. Neimeyer
December 2008

Selected Poems

Crossing the Unknown Sea, 2007, acrylic and mixed media
Lisa Jennings

The Art of Longing

Those of us who have driven
the long cold road alone
have watched the thin line
of trees, frosted white,
slipping behind

like memories.
We know the pull
of something unseen
beyond the reach of dry eyes,
fixed, blinking

at the distant mist.
We ride the road
with our lonely ghosts,
unwavering in their devotion
like penitents at the altar

of our grief.
This is how we perfect
the art of longing,
learn to nurse the hurt,
refuse the fullness

of this world.
For now, we keep driving,
lean into the dimming light,
lean further toward
winter's receding horizon,

and away from arrival.

Perlen Nucleus, 2003, mixed media
Sigrun Menzel

The Meeting

1. The Voice

There is a voice
that is ours
and not ours.
It rises up
from the deep well of being,
lets its shape be seen

indistinctly, like a manta
gliding closer, closer,
still silent, shimmering,
as seen from the surface.
Your tremors will confirm
that it is there.

2. The Coming

Your thrashing
will not bring it.
It answers the call
of quiet, the still heart,
resting between beats.

If you close your eyes
you will sense its coming.
Already it stands
on the threshold,
arrived unbidden
for the room made ready.

If you lift your gaze
to its face and bid it
enter, it will step in,
follow you
through all the rooms
of your house.
It is the only guest
who will fill the space

and make it larger.
It is the grandparent
you have always needed.

3. *The Dialogue*

You ask it why
it has come to you.

It answers, *It is you*
who have come to me.
I am the one who does not move,
who is always waiting.

You ask it what it waits for.

It says, *I wait for an opening,*
a pause in your speech
with others. My whisper
is low, but deep. It washes
though you, cleansing.

You ask what it washes.

It answers, *I wash away*
the misspent hours,
the extraneous attachments,

the needless pain.
Without them,
you will find a life of purpose.
Already you are shining.

4. The Gift

When it goes
it will leave you something
in a small box. You will find it
in the evening, open it
with trembling hands.
Touching it,
your breath will catch,
your eyes will flood with tears.
It is what you have always sought,
a globe of light,
pulsing, shifting form.

It is not yet a soul.

The Last Night

I sit here in this lodge
outfitted like a *ryokan*,
glance out beyond
the rice paper screen
to the turned earth,
the nimble shapes
of the *Edo* period garden
that cloaks the shoulder of hill.

Beyond the thin rustle
of crickets sawing off time,
beneath the tumble of water
over rocks pulled from the earth
like bones, the great machine
of Tokyo rumbles toward sleep.

This is the last night
of measured speech,
attuned ear, eager to catch
the words hidden in the *kanji*,
like runes.
It is the last night to live
into a life that can never be mine,
to grasp it with *hashi*, lift it
to taste in small bites,
exotic, delicate, a meal
to be eaten with the eyes.
Tomorrow, I will leave behind
the genuflection of the subtle bow,
the stock phrases that hold
the connection, the distance,
like a bridge.

What I will carry back with me
is the burnished bronze of autumn,
the bottomless depth of almond eyes,
the clean lines of the temple
of memory, its *tatami* mats
welcoming the caress of feet

that leave their shoes of hard habit
at the door.

In Situ 2, 2003, watercolor and pastel
Barbara Thompson

The Summer We Climbed Gaustadtoppen

for Finn

We limbered our limbs
on the lower slopes, pumped
for six hours through boggy
meadow, birch forests,
leaves greening into life.
On the sharp slide of scree
our veins pulsed with the streams
that corrugated the hills,
pulled us forward,
lifted into sky. Before us
the earth unfurled
like history.

On Gaustadtoppen you sought
the steep ascent, a kind of flight,
soaring on worn boots
above the thicket of wood,
the scent of fir.
Your sturdy legs paced the hike,
measured the height
with knowing strides.
The divots of grassland greeted
your arrival with wildflowers
small and bright
as clapping hands.

In ones and twos we slowed,
sought shade between the sun and snow.
But you surged on,
your weathered frame
clambering over boulder fields

strewn by an angry Norse god.
Fueled by something deeper
than ambition, you hungered
for the crest of rock that fled
before our steps like a horizon,

a high hard hook
to peg the memory.

Utah 24 Cliff, 2008, acrylic on canvas
Richard Knowles

Utah Triptych

1. Climbing down

The blaze of morning
ignites the cliffs,
evaporates the moon,
hanging ghostly as the coyote's howl.

It is time to begin the walk,
to be swallowed deep in the throat of rock,
time to climb down,
beneath history,
through the saline memory
of ancient seas
washing the earth
like a scouring hand.

Now the sea rises hot within us,
spills out,
seeks sand, sky,
the root of Utah juniper,
the cone of piñon pine.

It falls away
like a tear of lament.
It bleeds back
into the raised ribs of earth,
glowing yellow as bleached bones.

An old ache throbs still
beneath the pulse of words.
It pulls us
toward the vacancy of arches
fixing us with their empty stares.

The sun leans into us,
and we lean into the rocks.
Each footstep carries us
deeper into earth,
deeper into sky.

Like the desert,
we ripen toward subsistence.

Canyon, Colorado Plateau, 2007, watercolor
Richard Knowles

10 SEP 07

Raven

Raven, 2007, watercolor
Richard Knowles

2. Raven's roost

We thread through
the sand, the scree, the slickrock,
like shallow roots.
The land's emptiness seeps into us
with the ochre dust.

Like sentinels,
the great columns of stone
witness our coming,
our going,
impassive as the lizard's stare.
Life here withholds its secrets
from the unblinking eye of sun.

We stop to allow our words
to catch up with us,
receive the gift of shade
poured from the upturned bowl of rock.

From a crevice above,
a fragment of nothingness dislodges itself,
shrieks down on us
on a storm of wings.

The raven, its iridescence black as loss,
reclaims the harbor of night
in day's dead heat.
A dark animus,
it shadows our steps
as we depart,
harbinger of a midnight
that is not yet ours.

Collapsing Cliff 3, 2006, watercolor
Richard Knowles

3. *Escalante*

From the plains of rust red rock
the bluffs rise up,
verdant as an evening song.

The aspens and pines
have gathered the silence
and held it for our ears.
The woods fills our eyes
with the knowledge of green.
The desert is a shadow
we have forgotten.

Everything here is an act of creation.
Even the deer merely confirm
the presumption of life.

Like the stream that feeds
and bleeds the escarpment,
we pass through, and down,
to find an arid ground

to ease the letting go.

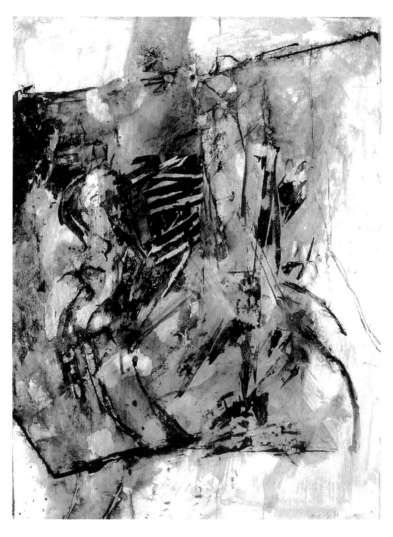

Newspaper Rock, 2007, acrylic on paper
Richard Knowles

Petroglyphs

There is a grace
in going free of talk,
swimming upstream
toward the source of words.
Before its birth,
all speech grew ripe in silence.

It was in that time
that sense sought stone,
that hands red as the rock
scraped patina from the cliff.
They found the shape of deer,
of snake,
sacred in their primal light.

They told the way
of coming and going,
traced the great circle
and the four known winds.
Gods too ancient for a living name
moved these hands
to define their form.

Now,
the canyon murmurs their chant,
a wind of words just beneath hearing.
The old hands with their tongues of flint
have long grown still,
turned to dust.
They have entrusted their ways
to the walls of rock
that lock tight their secrets
like an echo in the stone.

Room

Even the chair defines you
by your absence.
It lifts its arms
to embrace yours, opens its lap
to cup your form in its soft shape.
Without you,
it is an empty hand.

On the footstool the books
mill in their randomness,
forget their call to common purpose.
The pens on your desk
have bled dry of words.
Your tablet is a tombstone
without inscription.

This is how we are cast
by the long light of your shadow,
persist in our objective irrelevance.
Collectively, we have lost
the threads of memory,
of intention, dropped the beads
from time's limp string.
The clock's pulse
measures the silence
like a tin heart, registers
only hours *since*, never *until*.

Slowly we are hollowing
ourselves through our grief,
as rocks are carved by sand
in a hard wind.
When we have let go of enough
of what we were
and grow perfect in our nothingness,

we will at last find an end
to the yearning,
and finally

have room for you.

Sunday Morning, 1968, oil on canvas
Richard Knowles

Survivors

He has stopped trying
to grasp her remoteness
that he mistakes for calm,
this cooling that accompanies
the wintering of her grief.

Since their daughter's explosive
departure, its echo
like a slammed door,
she has pulled in, and in,
away from the pain,

away from him.
What he cannot know is how
she slips inside the sleeve
of her music, the lyrics
of angels
        touch
            return,
draws down into the bubble
of her hope.

Alone in her car,
the music builds a room
around her, around the room
a house through which
she strolls.
It is in the nursery
that she feels the peace,
rocks her child, rocks herself,
restores the bond.

Too soon, the car turns itself
into her drive, slides
into the vault of garage.

Her hand finds the latch,
pulls her out. She takes the steps
like a condemned man.

The forced hello fades,
yields to the distance.
She glances up at him,
sees the eyes,
the terrible mirrors,

and turns again to stone.

Mi Cabeza 9, 1998, collage on paper
Alfonso Garçia

Spirit

She was seven months in you
wrapped snug in your house of flesh
when she came to rest,
turned her face to the dark wall.
Beyond your high hard hope
you knew in your heart that she was gone,
this sliding shift of gravity
in your belly, in your bed.

You named her *Spirit*
because this is how she came to you—
there and not there,
a doll baby with eyes
painted shut. Instinctively,
your hands reach out,
grasp at air,
try to pull the light toward you,
into you, disperse the darkness.
A silent cipher, no one
can know what you have lost.

Now she stares at you
with the indifference of the angels
through the paper eyes, smiles
of baby pictures in your obstetrician's office,
the glazed gaze of newborns nursing
in restaurants at their mothers' breasts.
One after another, she tries on lives,
in the frames, in the arms of strangers.
She leaves each like a pair
of discarded shoes.

And so you seek her
in the misty maze to which she has retreated,
the shadow flash of dreams,

the sudden sightings of a body,
small and dark as a polished stone,
and as cold.
Left still on the couch,
found wrapped in a box,
she practices dying until it is perfected,
until you find a new way

of holding on.

1137 Christopher, 2007, black and white photograph
©Todd Hochberg

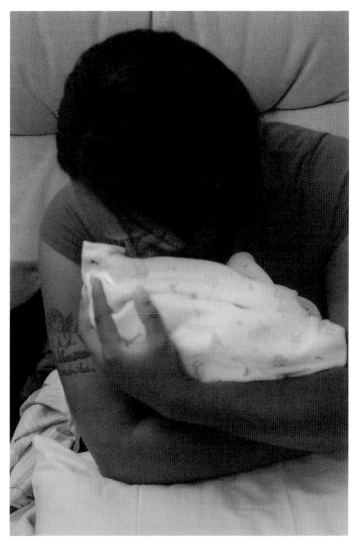

9097 Jeremiah, 2006, black and white photograph
©Todd Hochberg

Breakfast at the Retreat

> *to the survivors of Victims to Victory,*
> *and their quest to find grace beyond the homicide*
> *bereavement that is their common bond*

The clean round tables gather the women
like open palms, call them together
for the morning meal.
Night's grasp still holds them
in silence, like the still-fresh graves
that hold their husbands, their babies,
their lives.

To strengthen themselves
to tell the story again,
suture the wounds in group,
they take their plates,
find their place,
feel the always-empty chair
for each seat filled.

A woman with moist eyes
and a blue tattoo of her daughter
on her arm lifts the white jar,
pours sugar on her grits, forks in
the scrambled egg.

It's a Black thing, her Aunt Ethel explains,
a way to have something sweet
when your life is poor.

Send-off

The dead linger around us,
stand at the shore
ready to push off
in their slow boats.
They finger the mooring line,
cast an eye to the sky
grey with rain. They feel
the ebb tide coming for them,
drawing them away
like forgetting.

They wait, patient as pilgrims,
for our thick hold to weaken,
arms to fall. They yearn to slip free
of the tight knot of our grief,
seek the silence beyond our piercing sobs.
They know in their bones
we will not lift the anchor,
hoist the sail. They bear the farewell
as a final duty.

We reach for their thin hands,
clutch their skirts, tug their sleeves.
We seek the refuge of their limp arms
as a ship steers toward harbor
in a storm. They hold our past
in their vacant eyes. Our future
is sealed behind their lips. We cannot bear
the endless present.

They sense the call to board their vessels
like the screech of distant gulls. They feel
the tremble in our fingers, hear
the gathering quiet
in our wracked gasps. They know

the months are doing their rhythmic work,
wearing us like waves. In the end
we will release them,
force a wan smile, raise an anxious palm

or join them in our time
to make the passage.

BetweenWorlds, 2007, acrylic and mixed media
Lisa Jennings

Mist

spikes up from the morning lake.
The ghosts of wheat
circle, circle,
trace lines in a labyrinth.

The day is still the birds'—
their shrill shouts carve
the sky into zones, the land
beneath their green towers
reduced to a trough of worms.

Nothing human has yet begun—
the rusted piers
and upturned boats
the archaeology of a vanished tribe.
Its absence pulls back the blanket
of meanings, the "what for"
of the interpreted world.
            Revealed,
the scene composes itself,
asks nothing, permits anything,
winds forward with its own rhythms.

It is as if the night
had drowned language,
the grey lake dissolving
all we have written or read.

And then, as insistent
as the birds' song,
a lone poet scratches out words
like insects in the grass,

as the wheat field of mist
falls before the thrasher's blade.

Wash, Surf 4, 2001, acrylic on paper
Richard Knowles

Remembering, 2006, oil pastel
Barbara Thompson

In a Strange Place

Sometimes I awake in a strange
place, a bed of down pillows,
the sudden silence of an air conditioner
cycling off. Before me I see the lines
of cast shadows, grey, black,
the inked map of a dreamt city, its streets
unwalked.

To one side, the wall of glass and sheer
drapes shimmers like a cloudbank
pregnant with storms. The cicada pitch
of traffic thrums, thrums with a mechanical
throb, the breaths of a city,
asleep.

Always in such awakening
I lie still, blanketed in anonymity,
vigilant as something new.
Sometimes I will lean with my ears
into the night, catalogue the sounds
like minerals, rocks, each in its own
small box.

Or else I will fall back,
drop into the cracked egg of sleep,
find the blue pool and dive down,
and down, back toward *her*, warm, soft,
her face luminous, remote, unreachable as a
new moon.

Wash, Storm f, 2001, acrylic on paper
Richard Knowles

Mariza

Song made flesh,
you light the night with your eyes,
their flash the pulse of summer lightening.
Trees sway in your hum,
await the coming storm.

The *fado* breaks from you
like a sudden gale.
In the swelling waves of your voice
the sea rises like passion,
falls hard upon the shore.

Siren of sadness,
you draw us in, submerge us
in your longing.
You fill us without resistance,
carry us sodden into silence,
your raised brow a hook,
the flicker of your smile a lure.

Helpless,
we open to you
as fish relinquish their endless night
for one short pull into day,
for one long shiver of feeling.

Ethics of Paint, 2007, acrylic on canvas
Richard Knowles

The Artist Speaks

When he stands holding
the microphone
like an unfamiliar brush,
only a small pool of quiet
spreads around him
in the exposition's din.

His words are soft,
diffuse as his beard,
eyes deflected,
unintelligible.

And all about him
the walls scream
the color of his art—
Amidst the Forest,
Three Passages—
lacquered windows
to another world.

Like the stained glass of a cathedral
the dozen pigmented panels
lift up their voices in chorus,
convey the power
to silence those whose eyes
are open to their song.

Poets' Workshop

We wash into the room
in waves, swirl around the table
in an eddy of words.
Tousled, outfitted
by the Salvation Army,
few of us could be mistaken
for managers.

Most bear notebooks, backpacks,
duffle bags bulging
with crumpled language,
lay our loads around
the common table.

Slowly the work fans out,
oversized cards
in a low-stakes game.
Words spill from our bags,
from our mouths,
until I have the feeling
that the whole room is awash
in words—
poems clinging to the underside
of chairs like barnacles,
the walls *papier maché*,
the matted scraps of free verse
that came unglued
from their stanzas,
the table a huge book,
unopened.

We reach for our java
in identically-lettered Starbucks cups,
sip our espresso haiku,
linger over our French Vanilla sonnet,

bolt down our hard realism, black.
In a moment I am Ishmael,
wandering in a sea of verse,
the workshop leader a driven Ahab,
winced eyes scanning
the horizon of table top
for the Great White Whale.

My own poem surfaces,
and all eyes dart
to the movement,

each poised pen and pencil
a tiny harpoon.

Wash, Storm c, 2001, acrylic on paper
Richard Knowles

Nautilus, 2008, acrylic on canvas
Richard Knowles

Dog Days

August
and the long days
hollow themselves like ovens,
the whole town a loaf
on a slow bake,
timer broken.

Leaf by leaf
the dogwoods and azaleas
relinquish their seasonal hope,
their autumnal ambition
dried up with their juices.
With each day
they become more like
tattered parchment,
the words bleached yellow
as bones. They have found a way
to end the cycle
without winter's straitening,
a kind of suicide at the apex,
before the fall.

They call these *dog days*,
but the dogs refuse them.
Prodded to do their duty,
the hounds and beagles
stumble into the streets
as on a forced march.
Their tongues droop
in limp submission,
so many pink flags
of surrender.

Only the poets
are drawn to the heat,
seek its strict discipline,
require the glare
to pare their words.
They wait,
alert as lizards,
for the odd particular
that will seize the moment
like a flashbulb,
freeze the frame.
The incessant buzz stops.
A fly finds release
in the cool of the writer's
Grand Marnier, drifts
into the poem, and sacrifices itself

for art.

Crawdads

School's out.
The map of days
unrolls before Greg and me,
its trails and streams
our summer odyssey.
We beat the pavement
down Country Lane,
turn left on Betty Drive,
drop down into the low slope
beyond the rusted eyes
of mailboxes into an oasis
of shade, ferns and mud.

The cool water from the culvert
feeds the brook
where we kneel like penitents,
eyes tracing the quick blink
shooting under stones.

We fight over roles,
I win, hold the jar,
lift the flat rock. Greg risks
the goose-bump tickle
of needle feet, the pinch
of tiny claws.
Four small hands
do their wet work,
taking turns, filling
the Kosher containers with life
sparkling like fireflies.

A stick snaps.
We turn,
our sanctuary invaded.
The big boys, Protestants,

loom ape-like in the long shadows
of their leers.
Hey Catholic, the farm boy slurs,
what'd happen if I dropped
this here jar, hoisting our new pets
over the anvil rock.
It would break, I say,
eyes locked, lips tight,
my diction
sharp as knives.
His eyes dart
like crawdads to his gang.
Oh man, he blusters,
Who cares about these anyway,
sets down the jar
with a *C'mon* to his troops.

As we lose the crunch
of their Keds,
we laugh, leave,

and add a purple salamander
to our catch
on our hike home.

World XLI, 2006, watercolor
Richard Knowles

When We Had Them

When we conceived them
we were lost in bliss
or need, feverish
with the heat of merging.
Even if we reached
beyond ourselves
to a life that was theirs,
we sought only fruition,
the seed planted.

We did not think
as we carried them to fullness
of what would pass
when we had them,
delivered them shivering
into this world.

We did not pause
to contemplate the pain
that would chasten them,
the yearning
that would consume them,
the hard knowledge
that would make them whole.

And we did not imagine
that the thin arm
laid across our chest in sleep
would one day lift us close,
release us in our frailty
when we ourselves had learned
all that hardship and love
had to teach,
and fell free

of the cycle of care.

Mi Cabeza 5, 1998, collage on paper
Alfonso Garçia

Green Bell Pepper, 2008, watercolor
Richard Knowles

Disposal

Does your garbage disposal work,
asked my wife,
innocent of her sister's home.
It does, she replied,
but I hate it.
But it does work, she conceded.

She longed, she explained,
for a disposal worthy of the name,
one that could handle cut lemons.
Hers, she said,
struggled with cooked noodles.

Together, we worked to recall
the catechism of the kitchen,
the mythology of coffee grounds,
        disposed,
cleansing the blades that spun them,
or perhaps sharpening them
in some paradoxical dance
of grounds and steel.

And the sacrament of cold water,
or was it hot,
to flush the swirling font,
redeem the dregs of dinner,
transfigured by the rite.

But we, lapsed acolytes,
could access only mumbled vows,
unworthy of the gift

of transubstantiation.

Airport

It's 4 p.m., and for three hours
the counters and checkpoints
have been organizing the time.
They process us like products
on conveyors, sort and ship
to destinations. Overhead,
the high arches of girders fly
skyward, lift our hopes
beyond expectations. Down here,
we shuffle on etched granite,
herd through inspections.

Aboard, I gaze out at a day
that could be anywhere,
but is nowhere,
hear the absent news
of the mechanic tending
this bird's reluctant wing.
It is raining outside the portholes,
a tear running down the cheek of window
for everyone I will ever love.
The tarmac gathers the sadness,
its gray expanse the color of forgetting.
The worm of jetway
has detached its thick lips
from the hull, pulled back
to a respectful distance to await
the departure of its beloved.

Finally, over my right shoulder
a voice that knows my name
speaks it with Asian exactness.
I turn, drawn to the glowing lantern
of her face, and order the beef,
for later, when my heart lifts
toward home.

Viaje 4, 2008, cut steel
Alfonso Garçia

Cleaning Fish

Her perpendicular eye finds my own.
     End this, it says,
in a liquid language silent as the sea.

I wield the knife
like the swift gift of the shark.

My woman's hands,
burned dry by the chemo,
move as if attached to other arms.
The left, assured, clasps her trembling form.
The right, uncertain,
opens her white flesh,
marbled through with crimson strands.

The eggs I remove, the scales I work free.
     She is readied for the pan.

Pink ribbons, like her veins,
thread through our family line,
link the soft bodies of my mother,
     my sister,
          myself—
Weedy wombs, overfull, become
lagoons for the kelpy strands.

Few but the dying know
the peace of resignation.
With surgical precision, we
excise the unneeded tissue from life,
scrape clean the arteries of purpose,
the nerves of electric connection.
Emptied of ambitions,
we are hollowed mouths
opened to cup the flowing water—

caught fish on a stringer
pegged tight at shore's edge.

Shiva III, 1989, oil on canvas
Richard Knowles

Blood Test, 2007, watercolor
Richard Knowles

Tumor

for Gloria, three years living with cancer

No one knows when it began,
its history wrapped in a coded language,
like that of a small tribe subsisting
in the jungle of your body.
With spears and darts
it continues the hunt,
grows its domain.

You monitor it at a distance,
from the cockpit of the CAT scan
flying overhead. You match
its patience with yours, watch
the slow swell of its edges, its culture
ripening.
The doctors observe it with ritual interest,
these armchair anthropologists
in their cool rooms.

A millimeter at a time
you are learning the hard art
of coexistence. To live,
it must convert you,
cell after cell. Your frail body
knows it cannot suffer its absence.

And so there is only waiting,
the pressed patience of the border guard.
You breathe in small gasps,
eyes darting from the frontier to the clock,
its spider-leg hands trembling
with your own.

January Complexity, 2008, acrylic on canvas
Richard Knowles

Coal Town Hospice

On the banks of the Ohio,
far from the namable places,
the town squats, wounded.
The sturdy girders
of the bridges carry cars
away, away,
across the brown expanse of river
bleeding these hills,
across the tracks of the C&X coursing
with their loads of coke
and steel. In the pre-dawn drizzle
Main Street stands empty
as the stores, their vacant eyes
leaking the dreams
of grandfathers.

On either end of town tower
the Goliaths of the plant, the refinery.
They announce the descent
into this valley, bar the exit,
squelch hope with belching fumes.
Between them the town crouches,
subservient.

There is still work here,
deposits to be made
to bank accounts,
            to lungs.
The cancer sends its metastases
winding down the wide streets,
the back alleys.

The eager tendrils find the unstopped
cracks under doors, the open
windows, mouths. For the young,
there is one sure way
out.

It is here that hospice
does its dark work,
lays its light hand
on laboring chests.
The plants have set down roots
in the furrowed brows,
sewn seeds of need
in the fertile flesh. Questions seep
like oil from the pores.

Like history,
nurses have no answers to give.
They fill the beds, fill the bags
hanging on steel poles,
coax the anodyne
into collapsing veins.
With each loss, chaplains
suture the wounds with familiar verse,
lay the dead to rest in the scarred soil.
Social workers apply their gentle press
to the bereaved, nudge them back to life,

back to the factories. In the end,
the survivors carry the memory
on their bent shoulders,
feel the heavy hand of obligation
that follows them to the furnaces,
to their homes,

like grief.

The Life Aquatic

The place to sleep
is in the bow of a boat,
far forward, below deck,
almost at the water line.

There, at the precise intersection
of two worlds, you will be held
in the soft arms of the lake or sea,
feel the rocking, rhythmic,
repeating the beating of your heart,
the pulsing of your blood.

Only yesterday in night's dark cradle
I became a fetus in his mother's body,
as she was strolling, or making love,
lulled by the hollow amniotic thunking
of the waves upon the hull.

It is a deep liquid instinct
locked in every cell
that convinces me that we evolved
from something aquatic,
crawled reluctant onto land,
lost our way back.

Of all the ways that we can die,
drowning would not be the worst,
slipping under again,
like a flying fish,
into the primal medium
after a brief plunge into sun.

It must come as relief
to drop our ridiculous insistence
on puffing out words

with small breaths,
to let go the fraught quest
for bipedal balance
on the rocky earth.

I imagine that last great release
of air, like a galaxy of silver planets
rising toward the light,
a final salute to gravity's slow pull.

And I can sense the sinking,
dropping down into the deep,
certain affection of the water,
enclosing me like a womb,
inviting a reverse ontogeny,
my cells joining, rather than dividing,
simplifying in geometric regression
toward a unity

before the separation began.

Swimmer in Red Dress, 1986, oil on canvas
Richard Knowles

L'Ulmet

for Valeria and Carlo

From four lands
we have gathered here,
in this *ristorante*
with the Milanese name,
a tree untranslatable
into anything we know.

In this cozy place
friendship is planted,
takes root,
is cultivated, grows,
is celebrated with wine.
The green walls are a forest
for the soul, the stories
paths we walk together,
their only destination
to find the next trail.

We have stepped into this glen
from the bustle of the city,
its streets teeming with cars
like locusts eating time.
          Inside, we slow
to a different pace,
a saunter, an amble
in four languages—
the steady steps of English,
quick clips of *italiano*, *español*.
the soft shuffle of *catalan*.

We live in this moment
as a tree lives in rich soil,
is nurtured by the happy accident

of rain, leafs into sun
with a thousand opening hands.
We know that the seasons change,
that leaves brown and fall.
But for now, the calendar
stands open only to late spring,
our raised glasses
like buttercups
along the trail.

Trilogy I The Green Road, 2008, acrylic and mixed media
Lisa Jennings

Travelers

You know the lucky thing about my hip replacement?
she asked, not waiting for the answer.
It made me think about advance directives,
my living will, how I'd like to die.

Yeah, he said, her colleague
who chatted amiably with death
each day, like two old men
playing checkers in the park.
I know what you mean.

This is how it is
with the nurses, doctors, therapists
who walk down the halls of dying
as through the home of a relative,
pausing to leaf through the *Geographic*,
or straighten a family photograph on the wall.

They have earned their ease
the hard way,
learned to reach through the bramble
to find the fruit, add weight
to the rusty pail.

They have not so much grown inured
to pain as they have learned to savor it,
taste the sweetness in the grapefruit's bite,
feel the glow of a day's hard toil.

In the end, we need them
as we need seasoned travelers
met in an unfamiliar land.
They greet us on the steep trail,
in the twisting streets, point the way
to a good *taverna*, trace the path home.

Most of all, they help us
parse the dark syllables in our hearts,
bare them,

and seek cleansing
in the gathering storm.

The Eternal Circle, 2007, acrylic and mixed media
Lisa Jennings

Proof